02/06/2018

NORTH KOREA
TODAY

BY KATHRYN HULICK

CONTENT CONSULTANT

DR. ROBERT E. KELLY
PROFESSOR
DEPARTMENT OF POLITICAL SCIENCE AND DIPLOMACY
PUSAN NATIONAL UNIVERSITY, BUSAN, SOUTH KOREA

Essential Library

An Imprint of Abdo Publishing | abdopublishing.com

abdopublishing.com

Published by Abdo Publishing, a division of ABDO, PO Box 398166, Minneapolis, Minnesota 55439. Copyright © 2018 by Abdo Consulting Group, Inc. International copyrights reserved in all countries. No part of this book may be reproduced in any form without written permission from the publisher. Essential Library™ is a trademark and logo of Abdo Publishing.

Printed in the United States of America, North Mankato, Minnesota
102017
012018

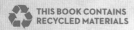

Cover Photo: STR/AFP/Getty Images
Interior Photos: Jon Chol Jin/AP Images, 4–5; Wong Maye-E/AP Images, 8, 40–41, 42; DigitalGlobe/38 North/Getty Images, 12; US Army, 14–15; Corbis Historical/Getty Images, 16–17; AP Images, 18, 28; Gene Herrick/AP Images, 23; Korean Central News Agency/Korea News Service/AP Images, 26–27, 52–53; Eric Lafforgue/Gamma-Rapho/Getty Images, 32; HO/WFP/AP Images, 37; Katsumi Kasahara/AP Images, 45; Kyodo/AP Images, 49; B. K. Bangash/AP Images, 55; Arnulfo Franco/AP Images, 60; Saul Loeb/AP Images, 62; AFP PHOTO/KCNA VIA KNS/STR/AFP/Getty Images, 64–65; Doug Mills/AP Images, 69; Kim Kwang Hyon/AP Images, 74–75, 83; Ed Jones/AFP/Getty Images, 78; Viktoria Gaman/Shutterstock Images, 84–85; Lee Jin-man/AP Images, 87; Daniel Chan/AP Images, 90–91; Staff Sgt. Jonathan Fowler/US Air Force, 93; Pablo Martinez Monsivais/AP Images, 96

Editor: Arnold Ringstad
Series Designer: Maggie Villaume

Publisher's Cataloging-in-Publication Data

Names: Hulick, Kathryn, author.
Title: North Korea today / by Kathryn Hulick.
Description: Minneapolis, Minnesota : Abdo Publishing, 2018. | Series: Special reports | Includes bibliographic references and index.
Identifiers: LCCN 2017946872 | ISBN 9781532113345 (lib.bdg.) | ISBN 9781532152221 (ebook)
Subjects: LCSH: United States--Foreign relations--Korea (North)--Juvenile literature. | Nuclear arms control--Verification--Korea (North)--Juvenile literature. | Diplomatic relations--Juvenile literature. | Nuclear nonproliferation--Juvenile literature.
Classification: DDC 327.5193--dc23
LC record available at https://lccn.loc.gov/2017946872

CONTENTS

CHAPTER ONE

BOMB
THREAT

A missile flies through the air, crossing the globe from North Korea to the United States of America. It slams into Washington, DC, its nuclear warhead exploding in a red mushroom cloud and devastating the city and its surroundings. Such an act of war seems unimaginable to many Americans. But this exact scene played out in a propaganda video posted to YouTube in March 2016. A North Korean website run by the country's government created the video, which featured computer-animated scenes of a nuclear strike on the United States and a burning US flag. The video also showed tests of real missiles and other weapons. Some of the Korean text superimposed over the video translates to: "If the American

Anti-US propaganda is a feature of daily life in North Korea.

imperialists provoke us a bit, we will not hesitate to slap them with a pre-emptive nuclear strike. . . . The United States must choose! It's up to you whether the nation called the United States exists on this planet or not."[1]

Earlier that month, the same website had boasted that North Korea had a hydrogen bomb that could wipe out Manhattan. "If this H-bomb were to be mounted on an intercontinental ballistic missile and fall on Manhattan in New York City, all the people there would be killed immediately and the city would burn down to ashes," said the article.[2] North Korea has made such threats before. The country has been promising to wipe out its enemies with nuclear strikes since the late 1990s and early 2000s. One of the most regularly repeated threats involves blowing up Seoul, the capital city of South Korea. In April 2017, a North Korean newspaper stated that the country's army had its nuclear arsenal aimed at US military bases in South Korea, on islands in the Pacific Ocean, and on the US mainland.

"[NORTH KOREA NEEDS] TO GET THE NUCLEAR WARHEADS DEPLOYED FOR NATIONAL DEFENSE ALWAYS ON STANDBY SO AS TO BE FIRED ANY MOMENT."[3]

—KIM JONG-UN, LEADER OF NORTH KOREA

No nuclear strikes have actually occurred. And since North Korea has been making threats for decades without acting on them, the world tends to shrug off the disturbing videos and articles. "If you follow North Korean media you constantly see bellicose language directed against the US and South Korea and occasionally Japan is thrown in there, and it's hard to know what to take seriously," says John Delury of Yonsei University in South Korea.[4] However, North Korea's threatening behavior goes beyond propaganda. The country has also built up a nuclear arsenal and tested weapons technology in violation of international law.

EXPLOSIVE POWER

North Korea's official name is the Democratic People's Republic of Korea, or the DPRK. The country was founded on September 9, 1948. Approximately the same size as the state of New York, North Korea is located on a peninsula extending from Eastern Asia, bordering China to the north and South Korea to the south. The leader, Kim Jong-un, heads a communist government that tightly controls its population. North Korea's 25 million people are subject to malnutrition, poor living conditions, and even forced labor. Travel is restricted and communications are censored and monitored.

Corruption permeates the North Korean government. In 2016, Transparency International, a group that scores countries on corruption, ranked North Korea the third most corrupt country in the world. Kim Jong-un is the latest member of the Kim family to hold power, and his reach is extreme. His regime controls all media and communications, restricts the population's travel, and maintains a strong military despite the fact that many people living in North Korea don't have access to basic necessities. The Kim dynasty fears that the rest of the world is out to destroy the regime. This paranoia has

North Korean dictator Kim Jong-un took power in 2011 following the death of his father, Kim Jong-il.

prompted the country to pour its resources into military development and continually flaunt its military might.

In 2005, the Korean Central News Agency released a statement saying that the country had "manufactured nukes for self-defense."[5] The statement claimed that US president George W. Bush was attempting to isolate and stifle North Korea, and that the country needed nuclear weapons to ensure its survival. A year later, an underground explosion rattled the earth in northeastern North Korea. That first explosion wasn't huge by nuclear weapons standards. But it proved that the country had become a nuclear power.

Nuclear weapons exploit the energy contained within the nucleus of an atom. Splitting apart particles in the nucleus, a process called fission, or joining them together, a process called fusion, releases a burst of energy. When many atoms split or fuse in quick succession, the result can be a devastating blast with enough power to destroy a large portion of a city. A typical nuclear weapon in the US arsenal delivers hundreds of kilotons of explosive power. One kiloton is equal to 1,000 short tons (907 metric tons) of the explosive material TNT. North Korea's first test blast exploded with less than 1 kiloton of power. Some believe the weapon may not have functioned properly, despite North Korea's claims that the test was a complete success. The testing didn't stop there. North Korea detonated nuclear bombs in 2009, in 2013, and twice in 2016. By 2016, the power of the blast had increased to 9 kilotons.

A powerful nuclear weapon isn't much use unless North Korea can deliver it to a desired target. Alongside its nuclear tests, the country has been testing rocket and missile technology. A small nuclear bomb could be fitted onto the tip of a missile with the ability to fly thousands of miles and hit a specified target. Such a missile may be launched from the ground or from a submarine. North Korea has proved through numerous tests that it

THE ULTIMATE WEAPON

In January 2016, North Korea set off an explosion of approximately 9 kilotons. The country claimed it had detonated a hydrogen bomb, but scientists were skeptical. A hydrogen bomb, also called a thermonuclear weapon, is the most destructive nuclear device in existence. It combines the power of both fission and fusion. A regular atomic bomb explodes due to a runaway chain of fission reactions. In a hydrogen bomb, this fission explosion forces a second stage of the bomb—which contains hydrogen fuel—to implode and undergo fusion, releasing even more destructive power. When the United States tested a hydrogen bomb in 1954, the blast yielded 14.8 megatons of energy.[6] North Korea's test explosion wasn't big enough to be a two-stage thermonuclear weapon. Either the claim was a bluff, or the country tested a less powerful version of the weapon.

has short-range missiles which could reach most of South Korea and Japan. It is also developing intercontinental ballistic missiles, which could reach targets in the continental United States.

RULE BREAKER

Every one of North Korea's nuclear and missile tests has violated international laws and treaties that govern the use of military force. The United Nations (UN) Security Council, an international organization tasked with maintaining peace and security throughout the world, has unanimously passed numerous resolutions in response to North Korea's nuclear tests. Each resolution condemns the test and imposes sanctions on the country. These sanctions are punishments intended to make it difficult for North Korea to continue to develop weapons. Some sanctions limit or prevent trade in certain materials and technology, allowing cargo heading for the country to be searched. Others put limits on travel and spending for people suspected of being involved in the nuclear program. The United States has also imposed its own sanctions on North Korea directly.

Fuel/oxidizer building

Exhaust deflector filled with rain water

Fuel/oxidizer building

Launch pad foundation

Gantry tower foundation

Control Building

Analysts examine satellite photos of North Korean facilities to estimate the progress of missile and weapons programs.

Despite the resolutions and sanctions, North Korea has continued to develop nuclear weapons and missile technology. Direct evidence about the size of North Korea's nuclear arsenal is very difficult to come by due to the country's extreme secrecy and isolation. No one outside of North Korea knows exactly how many weapons the country has on hand. However, experts in nuclear technology can make educated guesses based on the information that is available, including satellite imagery of nuclear facilities. As of 2016, the Institute for Science and International Security estimates that North Korea has between 13 and 30 nuclear weapons, and is actively building more. The size of the arsenal could approach 50 weapons by 2020.[7]

In the past, countries such as the United States have largely ignored North Korea and its threats. Its bombs simply weren't powerful enough or its missiles far-reaching enough to pose a real danger. Plus, an attack on the United States would be suicidal. The larger country would almost certainly retaliate with weapons powerful enough to completely devastate North Korea. But North Korea's power is growing. When President Donald Trump took office in January 2017, his predecessor, Barack Obama, warned him that the most urgent problem he was likely to face was the situation with North Korea. In April 2017, US secretary of state Rex Tillerson urged action on this situation. "Failing to act now on the most pressing security issue in the world may bring catastrophic consequences," he said.[8]

"FAR FROM ACHIEVING ITS STATED NATIONAL SECURITY AND ECONOMIC DEVELOPMENT GOALS, NORTH KOREA'S PROVOCATIVE AND DESTABILIZING ACTIONS HAVE INSTEAD SERVED TO ISOLATE AND IMPOVERISH ITS PEOPLE THROUGH ITS RELENTLESS PURSUIT OF NUCLEAR WEAPONS AND BALLISTIC MISSILE CAPABILITIES."[9]

—PRESIDENT BARACK OBAMA, SEPTEMBER 2016

FROM THE HEADLINES

THE UNITED STATES PREPARES FOR A POTENTIAL WAR

In response to North Korea's threats and missile tests, the United States has installed an advanced missile system in South Korea. The system, called the Terminal High Altitude Area Defense missile system, or THAAD, became operational in May 2017. The goal of the system is to detect the launch of an enemy missile, then fire a missile to intercept it in midair, destroying the enemy missile before it can reach its target. The United States has also sent warships to South Korea, including the nuclear submarine USS *Michigan* and an aircraft carrier. "The threat of a North Korean nuclear attack on Seoul or Tokyo is real, and it is likely only a matter of time before North Korea develops the capability to strike the US mainland," said US secretary of state Rex Tillerson.[10]

The THAAD system and warships angered North Korea. "We will make the US fully accountable for the catastrophic consequences that may be brought about by its high-handed and outrageous acts," read a statement from North Korean officials in response

THAAD underwent years of testing and development before being deployed in South Korea in 2017.

to the deployment of US warships." China opposes the THAAD system, saying that it could be used to spy on their country. Hundreds of South Koreans have protested the system as well. They are concerned that it might provoke an attack.

CHAPTER TWO

A NUCLEAR WORLD

n the 1940s and 1950s, the events that would eventually lead to today's confrontations in North Korea were set into motion. During this era, the atomic bomb was invented and Korea was split in two. The advent of nuclear weapons set the tone for the next several decades of international relations. The division of Korea resulted in a war followed by a long, intense stalemate. All these tensions continue to be felt in the 2010s.

On August 6, 1945, a US B-29 bomber flew over Hiroshima, Japan. Suddenly, a brilliant orange and red cloud mushroomed over the city. It was an atomic explosion, and it obliterated the city. Three days later, another atomic bomb destroyed much of Nagasaki,

Extensive weapons testing was carried out in the early years of the atomic age.

Japan. The center of each explosion burned hotter than the sun, scorching the ground, melting metal, and setting off blazing fires. Shockwaves from the explosions ripped through the cities like powerful hurricanes. More than 150,000 people lost their lives in these attacks. Some died immediately from the fireball and shockwave. Others perished after suffering from terrible burns, injuries, or radiation sickness, which is caused by harmful particles released during nuclear reactions. Weeks after the destruction of Hiroshima and Nagasaki, Japan surrendered to the United States. World War II (1939–1945) was finally over.

Few structures remained standing in Hiroshima following the city's atomic bombing.

THE POWER SPREADS

The advent of nuclear weapons technology began a new era in human history. A single leader with access to nuclear weapons could wipe entire cities off the map and kill hundreds of thousands of people in minutes. Since then, even more powerful nuclear weapons have been developed. The most destructive one by far is the hydrogen bomb. Also called a thermonuclear weapon, it is hundreds to thousands of times more powerful than the bombs dropped on Hiroshima and Nagasaki.

As nuclear technology has advanced, it has also spread to multiple countries. The United States was the first country to develop and drop a nuclear bomb. The Soviet Union soon followed, conducting its first nuclear test in 1949. Though the United States and the Soviet Union had been allies at the end of World War II, the relationship between the two countries quickly deteriorated after the war, leading to a power struggle called the Cold War that lasted until the late 1980s. During the Cold War, the democratic United States and communist Soviet Union each worried that the other would attack with nuclear weapons. As a result, these countries put a huge amount of money and effort into building enormous stockpiles of weapons. They also developed missile technology capable of delivering the bombs to specific targets. After the Soviet Union collapsed in the 1990s, its largest successor, Russia, took over its nuclear arsenal.

Other countries have felt compelled to arm themselves with nuclear weapons as well. By 2017, France, China, the United Kingdom, Pakistan, India, Israel, and North Korea had all joined the ranks of nuclear-armed nations. Some of these countries developed weapons to feel more secure in the face of international threats. Others wanted weapons for prestige, since a nuclear arsenal can help convey status as a world power.

However, plenty of wealthy, powerful countries do not have nuclear weapons. These countries are typically closely allied with one or more nuclear-armed nations that have promised protection. A number of international nonproliferation treaties and agreements have led countries that were working on developing nuclear weapons to end their programs. Other agreements have resulted in the reduction of the number of weapons in nuclear stockpiles. Since the 1980s, the total number of these weapons in the world has been falling. In 2017, there were approximately a quarter as many nuclear weapons in the world as in 1986, and the vast majority of these bombs belonged to the United States and Russia.

Despite the overall trend toward fewer nuclear weapons, these two countries still possess a terrifying amount of destructive power. Some experts estimate that the US nuclear stockpile alone could destroy life on Earth five times over. But ever since the end of World War II, the world's nuclear powers have refrained from using these weapons outside of testing. The bombs the United States dropped on Hiroshima and Nagasaki in 1945 remain the only two nuclear weapons ever used in war.

NUCLEAR WINTER

In a nuclear war, the most immediate danger would be the blast force, heat, and radiation. Even though these bombs would not incinerate every inch of the planet, no living creature would escape the effects of such a catastrophe. Each blast would fill the air with dust and start terrible fires that would spew out choking clouds of smoke. The dust and soot would darken the sky, blocking sunlight and cooling the surface of the Earth. Scientists have predicted that even a relatively small nuclear exchange involving around 100 atomic bombs of the size used on Hiroshima would likely lead to changes in temperature and rainfall that could result in widespread famines.

THE KOREAN WAR

However, the decades that have passed since 1945 have hardly been peaceful. As conflicts have broken out around the world, countries have been tempted to respond with nuclear weapons. The Korean War (1950–1953) became the first such conflict to test the practical applications of nuclear power. During World War II, Japan had seized control of Korea. When the war ended, Japan lost control of Korea, and the nation was divided up. The United States occupied the south and helped set up a democracy, while the Soviet Union occupied the north and established a communist government. By 1949, the new nations began to attack each other. Each side felt that it was the one, true Korea.

On June 25, 1950, North Korea launched a full invasion of South Korea, taking over the southern capital of Seoul in less than a week. The UN, a union of world powers that had been established at the end of World War II with the goal of preventing another world war, held a meeting to decide what to do. The Soviet Union did not attend the meeting, and the countries present decided to assist

US forces launched an amphibious invasion of North Korea in late 1950.

South Korea. Soon, UN troops had pushed North Korean forces back across the border, almost all the way to China. By the fall of 1950, China had started sending in troops to assist North Korea, swinging the balance of the conflict yet again.

When the Korean War broke out, the United States was still the most advanced nuclear power. In the spring of 1951, the United States sent nuclear weapons and airplanes capable of carrying and dropping those weapons to Japan, a country just a short flight away from the Korean peninsula. Historians believe the United States came very close to dropping nuclear bombs on North Korea. But before that could happen, US president Harry Truman fired military commander Douglas MacArthur. Historians suspect MacArthur's desire to use nuclear weapons was part of the reason for his dismissal. After three years of fighting, a cease-fire agreement was reached in 1953. North Korea and South Korea would remain separate nations. No nuclear mushroom clouds rose above the peninsula during the conflict.

TOO POWERFUL TO USE

However, nuclear weapons don't need to explode to affect the actions of world leaders. Throughout the Korean War, the Cold War, and other conflicts, nuclear weapons have played an important role as a deterrent. Nuclear deterrence is the theory that possessing nuclear weapons helps prevent enemies from attacking, because such an attack would provoke an instant, deadly counterattack.

For example, by the 1960s, both the United States and the Soviet Union had missiles standing ready to launch at each other. A single command from either nation's leader could have set off a global catastrophe. They were at a stalemate. If either attacked, the other would be able to respond nearly instantly, ensuring that both would be destroyed. Although the threat of mutual destruction can help maintain a sort of peace, it's a very tenuous balance to maintain.

"IMAGINE A ROOM AWASH IN GASOLINE. AND THERE ARE TWO IMPLACABLE ENEMIES IN THAT ROOM. ONE OF THEM HAS 9,000 MATCHES. THE OTHER HAS 7,000 MATCHES. EACH OF THEM IS CONCERNED ABOUT WHO'S AHEAD, WHO'S STRONGER. WELL, THAT'S THE KIND OF SITUATION WE ARE ACTUALLY IN."[1]

—ASTRONOMER CARL SAGAN, ABC NEWS "VIEWPOINT," NOVEMBER 1983

CHAPTER THREE

THE ROGUE
STATE

T he Korean War did not leave a lasting impact on the people of the United States or most other Western nations. For this reason, the conflict is sometimes called "The Forgotten War." But in Korea, the war remains fresh in everyone's minds. Approximately 5 million people died, including at least 1 million North Korean soldiers and civilians. From the perspective of the outside world, North Korea started the war when it invaded South Korea, and the winner of the conflict was unclear. South Korea retained its independence, but North Korea also continued to exist.

However, North Koreans see history differently. They learn in school that South Korea and the United States attacked first, and North Korea had no choice but

Kim Il-sung, leader of North Korea from 1948 until his death in 1994, forced his citizens to revere him as partly divine.

to respond. They view the United States as an invading aggressor in the conflict, which they call the Fatherland Liberation War. Mina Yoon, who was raised in North Korea and escaped in 2010, says that she never even heard a single rumor that things might have happened differently. But then she left North Korea and started to relearn many of the things she'd been taught. "The truth about Korean War was the biggest surprise," she says.[1]

From the North Korean point of view, the United States already invaded once and might do so again. North Korea has viewed the United States as a terrible threat for more than 60 years. It has worried that the United States will try to force a regime change. At first, North Korea had

Many Korean refugees fled the North Korean army during the war.

the protection of the Soviet Union's nuclear arsenal. But when the Soviet Union collapsed, North Korea was left to its own devices. "North Korea lost its main protector. Its turn to developing nuclear weapons made a lot of sense," says Keir Lieber of Georgetown University.[2] Self-defense through nuclear deterrence is a key aspect of North Korea's nuclear program.

A CULT OF PERSONALITY

In the aftermath of the Korean War, North Korea received aid from both the Soviet Union and China. In the 1960s and 1970s, North Korea experienced its most productive years, outpacing South Korea in both agriculture and industry. But North Korea was also gradually losing touch with the rest of the world. The Kim family built up an ideology based on the concept of *Juche*, which means "self-reliance." Juche has its roots in communism, the theory at the heart of the governments of the Soviet Union and China at the time. But Kim Il-sung, the first leader of North Korea, added the idea of Juche to his style of government. He began to call himself the Great Leader and set out to establish a cult of personality.

The government presented a heroic, idealized image of him and his place in his country's history.

The idea that the United States started the Korean War is just one of many myths his regime established. It also erased the fact that the United States dropped two atomic bombs on Japan to end World War II. Instead, according to the myths about Kim, he was responsible for defeating the Japanese and ending the occupation of Korea. Yoon explains that the North Korean government works very diligently to spread only one version of the truth—a version that makes the ruling regime look strong and honorable. "It is really hard to get any information other than what the government wants the people to know," she says.[3]

In 1949, before the Korean War had even broken out, North Korea erected the first statue of Kim Il-sung. By 1992, more than

JUCHE

Kim Il-sung called his political ideology *Juche*, a Korean word that means "self-reliance." According to the official formulation of this philosophy, *Juche* is a socialist idea that means people must solve problems for themselves. However, in reality it has come to mean that the people must be absolutely loyal to their leaders, and that the country as a whole should not trust or rely on outsiders. The three main components of *Juche* are political independence, economic independence, and military independence. Kim Jong-il emphasized military independence in society with a policy he called Military First, which officially prioritized the military over everything else.

40,000 statues and monuments had been built to honor him. Kim purposefully rid the country of any belief system that might compete with his own. He executed or exiled opposing political leaders. He threw religious leaders in jail and destroyed thousands of Buddhist temples and Christian churches. The Great Leader became like a god to his people. "We were told that he crossed the river on a bridge of leaves and then he threw pine cones and they turned into grenades," says Ahn Hyeok, a former political prisoner in North Korea. "We heard this over and over, and we really believed that. So naturally we idolized him."[4] Jang Jin-sung, a poet who achieved a high rank in North Korea before he defected, described the Great Leader this way: "Our General's life is a continuous series of blessed miracles, incapable of being matched even by all our mortal lifetimes put together."[5] Kim Il-sung was supposedly partly human and partly divine, and ordinary North Koreans still strive to try to be like him.

FATHER, SON, AND GRANDSON

When Kim Il-sung passed away in 1994 from a heart attack, the entire country of North Korea fell into mourning.

Their sadness was most likely real, says Victor Cha, author of the book *The Impossible State.* "The people had been taught to love the Great Leader like their own mother and god, wrapped into one," he says.[6] Kim's son, Kim Jong-il, officially took over as dictator of North Korea in 1998. One of the first things he did was to declare his father the "eternal president" of North Korea. The elder Kim's body was preserved for all to see at a special mausoleum, and the younger Kim took on the title Dear Leader. Kim Jong-il also established a new calendar for North Korea. The calendar counts from the year of his father's birth in 1912. In North Korea, the year 2018 is Juche 107. Though the younger Kim was actually born in Russia, his people learn

Propaganda posters showing Kim Il-sung, *left*, and Kim Jong-il, *right*, are prominently displayed in North Korea.

that he was born on a sacred mountain in North Korea, and that a double rainbow and new star appeared in the sky to mark his birth. His biography, written by the regime, claims that Kim Jong-il got 11 holes-in-one on an 18-hole golf course.

Kim Jong-il passed away suddenly in December 2011, and his second son, Kim Jong-un, took over leadership of the country and the title of supreme leader. Just like his father and grandfather before him, the youngest Kim's official story makes him out to be a military expert and a genius. The international community knows very little about his actual upbringing and accomplishments. But his goals are clear. He has said repeatedly that he plans to continue to develop North Korea's nuclear capabilities.

The people of North Korea, meanwhile, are indoctrinated from a young age to trust, love, and obey their leaders. Statues and monuments aren't the only reminders. Pictures of the Kims hang in homes, offices, classrooms, and train cars. People must clean these pictures with a special cloth every day. They also wear pins with one or several of the leaders' likenesses. Televisions and radios broadcast only media approved by the regime, which is mostly propaganda praising the Kims and demonizing other countries, especially the United States, Japan, and South Korea. In school, children sing songs about the Kims and sometimes even play military games in which they attack wooden dummies of American soldiers. A poster hanging in a kindergarten reads: "Drive out the American imperialists. Let's reunify our fatherland."[7]

HIDDEN SUFFERING

During the 1990s, after the collapse of the Soviet Union, Kim Jong-il instituted a policy he called Military First, which elevated the military as the country's top priority. This policy of pouring all resources into building up the military had a severe effect on the general population. The Soviet Union's collapse also took away North Korea's main means of economic support. A series of droughts and floods compounded the issue, and the country went through a four-year period in the late 1990s known as the Great Famine. As many as

"THE REGIME FOUNDED BY KIM IL-SUNG IS A CULT POSSESSING INSTRUMENTS OF A NATION-STATE . . . [NORTH KOREA] IS, FROM ALMOST ANY PERSPECTIVE, THE WORST COUNTRY IN THE WORLD."[8]

—GORDON G. CHANG, AUTHOR OF *NUCLEAR SHOWDOWN: NORTH KOREA TAKES ON THE WORLD*

MORE TO THE
STORY

FLEEING FAMINE

When Yeonmi Park was nine years old, she watched as her best friend's mother was shot to death. Her crime was watching South Korean movies and lending them to friends. The young girl also witnessed emaciated, dying people lying in the streets during the Great Famine. Her family managed to stay fed thanks to her father's illegal business selling gold, silver, and nickel in China. But in 2002, he was caught and sent to prison, where he endured torture. His family lost their home, and Yeonmi had to eat grasshoppers and dragonflies. After three years, her father managed to bribe his way out and the family fled the country. They made it to China but discovered that life there was just as bad. "Even in China we were hungry," Yeonmi recalls. "There was no electricity. We couldn't pay for water."[9] Then, Yeonmi's father died, and she and her mother fled across the Gobi Desert into Mongolia. Finally, they connected with South Korean officials and made it to Seoul. Today, Yeonmi is an activist fighting to help her people.

three million people starved to death. The international community responded with humanitarian aid, but North Korea continually refused to cooperate with the foreign governments that were trying to help. Much of this aid never made it to the people who needed it most, as the military and other officials received money and food intended for the poor. Many humanitarian organizations have refused to operate in North Korea due to the corruption there. They worry that any aid they give will just end up funneled to the military.

Hunger and poverty continue to be an issue for North Koreans, who are taught that enduring suffering is a virtue. Under this mind-set, poverty is not a problem. Rather, it's necessary for the people to suffer in order for the state to thrive. The sacrifices of the people ensure the survival of the state that protects them. In 2016, the North Korean newspaper *Rodong Sinmun* warned citizens of the possibility of another famine, describing such an event as an "arduous march": "We may have to go on an arduous march, during which we will have to chew the roots of plants once again. . . . Even if we give up our lives, we should continue to show our loyalty to our leader, Kim Jong-un, until the end of our lives."[10] The 2016 Global Hunger Index estimates that 41.6 percent of the population is undernourished.[11]

If a North Korean tries to flee the country or speaks out against the government, he or she is taking a huge risk. Defectors may be tortured, executed, or sent to work in prison camps. The defector's parents, siblings, and other close relatives and friends may be punished as well, even if they did nothing wrong. These consequences make it difficult for most people to consider flight or revolution as possibilities.

The regime uses North Korea's caste system, known as *songbun*, as a tool to maintain control of the people.

The UN shipped vast quantities of rice to North Korea in 1996 in an effort to relieve the Great Famine.

Kim Il-sung divided the citizens into three classes, known as "core," "wavering," and "hostile."[12] The core group consisted of the people most loyal to the regime. These people enjoyed the most privileges. The wavering group consisted of laborers and other workers. The hostile group consisted of people who had helped the Japanese occupiers during World War II or who had opposed Kim when he took power. The regime moved many of these people to poverty-stricken northern areas of North Korea.

Under the songbun system, these classifications can be inherited. This means that they still dictate how many North Koreans live today. In times of famine, the regime has given its limited food supplies to the core classes first, allowing lower-class people to starve. The UN has called on North Korea to end this discrimination. In a 2014 report, it said North Korea should "end discrimination

LIFE IN THE PRISON CAMPS

Hundreds of thousands of people live in North Korea's prison camps. An inmate's day begins early in the morning and typically involves hours upon hours of grueling, dangerous labor such as mining, logging, or construction. Old or weak prisoners sew clothing or manufacture other goods. The workers must meet strict quotas. If they don't, they may face solitary confinement or torture. There is never enough food. One former prisoner describes what the experience was like: "We were always hungry and resorted to eating grass in spring. Three or four people died of malnutrition."[13]

against citizens on the basis of their perceived political loyalty or the socio-political background of their families."[14] However, the system remains firmly in place.

North Korea does its best to hide the human rights abuses happening within its borders. Official media show imagery of happy, healthy elite citizens living in the capital city of Pyongyang. In general, it's difficult to know whether any statement North Korea makes about its military, its government, or its people is true or not. This veil of propaganda coupled with an attitude of aggression toward the outside world has only reinforced North Korea's separation from the international community. Though China came to North Korea's aid during the Korean War and has been its strongest ally in the past, even this relationship has been strained by North Korea's continuing refusal to halt its weapons programs or reform its military and economic policies. At this point, North Korea is truly a rogue state. Its motivations are nearly impossible for outsiders to understand, and its actions are difficult to predict. It is a nation standing alone against the world.

CHAPTER FOUR

MILITARY
MIGHT

N orth Korea has been building up its military might for decades. From the ruling regime's point of view, a strong military equipped with nuclear weapons is essential to ensure the nation's continued existence. Plus, nuclear weapons bestow a kind of prestige. Only a few countries in the world have become nuclear powers, and North Korea is one of them. Though North Korea is a small, poor country, its weapons make it a significant international player.

The North Korean nuclear program is as much about national identity as it is about self-defense. Thanks to Kim Jong-il's policy of Military First, a strong military has become an object of devotion for the population. They believe in their military as a powerful

North Korea's military parades serve a propaganda purpose and are intended to be seen by people both inside and outside the country.

protector that keeps them safe and secure and take great pride in their military achievements. Kim Jong-un has said that nuclear weapons and missiles bring his country "dignity and national power."[1]

The military is a part of daily life in North Korea. Men must serve ten years in the military and women seven. They often refer to the Kims as General, and propaganda posters typically feature soldiers, missiles, and other military symbols. Despite North Korea's small size, the country has the fifth-biggest military in the world.[2] Grand military parades help bring the public together and demonstrate to the rest of the world the might of the regime.

The estimated size of North Korea's army is approximately one million soldiers.

TREMORS OF TROUBLE

North Korea's parades show off the size of the army and the variety of missiles and other weapons the country has built. In addition to these parades, the regime regularly boasts about its military capabilities in state-sponsored newspapers, television programs, and other media. But these boasts could be exaggerated, making it difficult to determine the truth about the actual destructive power of North Korea's arsenal. To try to get at the true status of the country's military, experts piece together clues from a variety of sources, including satellite images and data gathered during nuclear tests.

North Korea tests its nuclear weapons underground in tunnels dug beneath Mount Mantap at the Punggye-ri test site near the country's northeastern border with China. Detonating a nuclear warhead underground helps avoid the risk of radiation spreading in the atmosphere and sickening people and animals living nearby. It may seem that an underground explosion would be difficult to monitor or measure. But in fact, a nuclear explosion is too big to hide, even underground. These massive explosions produce earthquake-like tremors that travel through the ground. Scientists in the neighboring countries of China and South Korea have instruments set up to watch for such tremors. When they notice a particular pattern centered at North Korea's nuclear test site, they know that a bomb has exploded there. To confirm that the bomb was nuclear, air monitoring stations test for any radioactive isotopes that may have escaped from the tunnels. The strength of the vibrations determines the power of the blast. The most powerful explosion to date, from September 2017, produced an artificial earthquake with a magnitude estimated at 6.3, which likely translates to more than 100 kilotons of explosive power. That's much more damaging than the 15-kiloton atomic bomb that hit Hiroshima in 1945. Experts say that Mount Mantap could safely contain an explosion of up to 282 kilotons.

DISTANT REACH

Increasing the explosive power of nuclear bombs is one goal for North Korea's nuclear program, but arguably not the most important one. North Korea must be able to deliver its nuclear weapons to distant targets using

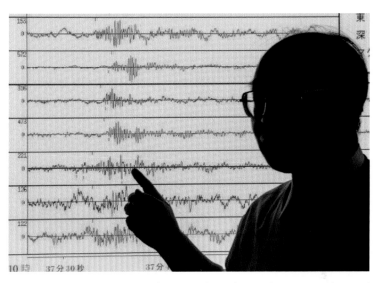

Japan and other nations in the region have detected seismic evidence of North Korea's nuclear tests.

missiles. A missile is a weapon that can propel itself through the air while using some sort of guidance system. North Korea currently has approximately 1,000 ballistic missiles of different types.[3] Most could only reach as far as South Korea or Japan, both close neighbors. The ultimate goal, though, is to build a missile with a much longer range, known as an intercontinental ballistic missile. This would give the country the ability to strike targets in North America.

In order to arm such a weapon with nuclear bombs, North Korea must build them small and light enough to travel inside the missile. "[A nuclear weapon] doesn't do the North Koreans much good if they have to put it

SOLID FUEL

In February 2017, North Korea test launched a mid-range missile. Though North Korea had tested this missile before, this time one important thing was different. This missile used solid fuel instead of liquid fuel. Liquid fuel is unstable, so it's not safe to store it on board the rocket. A convoy of trucks have to carry the fuel out to the rocket's location just before launch to fill it up. During this fueling period, international satellites have time to observe the activity and prepare a counterattack before the rocket is ready to fire. Solid fuel, on the other hand, is much more stable. This makes solid-fuel missiles easier to move, hide, and launch without very much warning.

in a truck," says Jeffrey Lewis of the Monterey Institute of International Studies.[4] This problem may have already been solved. Making a nuclear bomb smaller mostly involves tweaking the design to make the implosion more efficient. North Korea claimed that its 2013 nuclear test was a miniaturized device, and experts say it definitely could have been. In addition, a propaganda photograph from April 2017 shows Kim Jong-un standing beside a shiny, silver sphere that is supposedly a miniaturized nuclear bomb. Experts aren't sure if the sphere is actually a real bomb, but they can tell that it's small enough to fit inside the nose cone of a missile.

To be effective, a bomb-laden missile must be able to reach its target. North Korea doesn't seem to be as close to solving this issue. The country has test launched dozens of missiles in 2016 and 2017, and many of these launches have ended in failure. The longest-range missile that North Korea has successfully tested is the Musudan, which launched eight times in 2016 with only one success, traveling approximately 250 miles (400 km).[5] A test launch of a similar missile in February 2017 also succeeded. The missile flew high up into the air, then landed 310 miles (500 km) away in the sea. When fired at a shallower angle, its range could extend up to 2,175 miles (3,500 km), far enough to reach US forces on the island of Guam in the Pacific Ocean.[6]

Two missile launches in April 2017 failed, and analysts have not yet determined what kinds of missiles were used for these tests. The failures have all either exploded in the sky or crashed into the sea soon after launch.

CYBERWARFARE

The standard approach to countering a missile strike is to blast the missile out of the air before it can hit its target. This is akin to hitting a bullet with a bullet, a tricky maneuver that can easily fail. It's especially difficult to intercept intercontinental missiles. When it comes to North Korea and Iran's nuclear programs, the United States has been pursuing another means of counterattack: trying to hack into the computer systems that control the missiles. "You can interfere with [the computer system] and keep them from ever launching it. Or if it does launch, send it off into the water in its opening moments," says David Sanger, a reporter and author of a book about cyberwarfare.[7] This program is very secretive, but some suspect a US cyberattack may have had something to do with North Korea's seven failed missile launches in 2016.

FROM THE
HEADLINES

SATELLITE LAUNCHED INTO SPACE

The space age in North Korea began in December 2012, when the country successfully launched a satellite into orbit around Earth. It repeated this feat in February 2016. North Korea insisted these were scientific satellites intended to perform peaceful tasks such as forecasting the weather and monitoring forests and farmland. After the 2016 launch, North Korean news announced, "Today's success is a proud result of scientific achievement and an exercise of our legitimate right to space. . . . The National Aerospace Development Administration plans to launch many more satellites following our national policy of focusing on the importance of science and technology."[8]

However, the United States and its allies suspected that the launches were actually intended to test technology for intercontinental missiles. The rocket motors, guidance software, and fuselages used to launch a satellite could also be used to fire a long-range missile. The UN Security Council condemned the launch. "It is deeply deplorable that the Democratic People's Republic of Korea has conducted a launch using ballistic missile

Technicians in North Korea's launch control room observed the rocket in preparation for the December 2012 launch.

technology in violation of relevant Security Council resolutions, said Secretary General Ban Ki-moon.[9]

Many headlines warned that these were missile launches in disguise. However, neither rocket was carrying any sort of weapon. Instead, they placed small satellites into orbit. These satellites may not be working properly, as they do not seem to have transmitted any data back to Earth.

North Korea has also been developing longer-range missiles, including the KN-08 and KN-14. Both would have ranges of 6,200 miles (10,000 km) or more—far enough to reach most of the United States. However, to fly this distance, the missile must travel into outer space and then drop back down into the atmosphere. If not designed properly, the missile will burn up on its way back down toward Earth. "You have to have a re-entry vehicle and design combination that is durable enough to survive the rigors of re-entry," says James Acton of the Carnegie Endowment for International Peace.[10] Accurately aiming the missile as it falls back to Earth is another difficult issue. North Korea has launched two satellites into space, likely in an attempt to test technology for intercontinental missile launches.

The April 2017 parade to mark the occasion of Kim Il-sung's birthday revealed two intercontinental missiles that hadn't been seen before, carried on huge trucks. The parade also introduced two gigantic missile canisters. These are massive, cylindrical devices used to launch large missiles. Soldiers, tanks, and floats surrounded by flag-waving people followed the missiles. One of the floats depicted missiles over planet Earth, along with doves and the words "for the peace and security of the world."[11] The event was bigger in scale than usual. "It's clear that North Korea wants to flex its military muscles," said Al-Jazeera reporter Nassir Abdulhaq after viewing the parade.[12] North Korea is hoping the rest of the world takes notice.

On July 4, 2017, North Korea successfully tested its first intercontinental ballistic missile. The missile, called the Hwasong-14, flew 578 miles (930 km) during a 37-minute flight, according to the South Korean and US militaries. It landed in the water between North Korea and Japan. Analysts believe such a missile could potentially reach the United States. Following the successful launch, the North Korean government described it as "a momentous event in the history of the country."[13] The development of the missile further complicated the confrontation between North Korea and the United States.

"THE UNITED STATES STRONGLY CONDEMNS NORTH KOREA'S LAUNCH OF AN INTERCONTINENTAL BALLISTIC MISSILE. TESTING AN ICBM REPRESENTS A NEW ESCALATION OF THE THREAT TO THE UNITED STATES, OUR ALLIES AND PARTNERS, THE REGION, AND THE WORLD."[14]

—US SECRETARY OF STATE REX TILLERSON, JULY 4, 2017

CHAPTER FIVE

A SECRET
MARKET

D espite North Korea's isolation from most of the world, the country has not developed its nuclear and missile technology entirely on its own. It has had help along the way from other countries, including the Soviet Union early on and Pakistan more recently. In addition, North Korea has sold guns, missiles, nuclear weapons technology, and fissile material to countries including Iran, Yemen, Libya, and Syria. This type of transaction is illegal and happens in secret. But North Korea, with its economy struggling since the collapse of the Soviet Union, believes it needs this illicit money. The sale of missiles and other weapons is likely one of the country's biggest sources of income.

Kim Il-sung, *left*, meets with Soviet leader Konstantin Chernenko in 1984.

THE BLACK MARKET

North Korea wasn't the first nation to sell weapons technology. In the 1970s, Pakistani nuclear scientist Abdul Qadeer Khan began working on a nuclear weapons program for his home country. Pakistan felt it needed the means to defend itself against its neighbor and rival India, which had tested its first atomic weapon in 1974. Through Khan's job at a nuclear fuel company in the Netherlands, he gained access to blueprints for an advanced device called a centrifuge that can be used to enrich uranium. He stole this information and returned to Pakistan.

As Khan worked toward Pakistan's goal of testing a nuclear bomb, he also began secretly selling sensitive materials to other countries, including Iran, Libya, and

SYRIA

Unrest broke out in Syria in 2011, when citizens began to protest against their president, Bashar al-Assad. The president responded with force, and a civil war broke out between the rebels and the ruling regime. Since then, an extremist group called the Islamic State and several world powers have gotten involved. An estimated 250,000 Syrians have lost their lives.[1] The horrific nature of this war has not stopped North Korea's leadership from selling guns and possibly even chemical weapons to Bashar al-Assad. Weapons experts have seen pictures of fighters in Syria carrying a type of machine gun made only in North Korea.

North Korea. An anonymous US official describes Khan's career as follows: "[Khan] develops a quite advanced nuclear arsenal. Then he throws the switch, reverses the flow and figures out how to sell the whole kit, right down to the bomb designs, to some of the world's worst governments."[2] In the early 1990s, Pakistan had developed nuclear weapons, though it didn't test one until 1998. But the nation still needed a missile that could carry these weapons. Over the next decade, North Korea provided Pakistan with prototypes of missiles that Khan's

Khan is a major figure in the history of nuclear proliferation.

laboratories could copy. In return, North Korea received prototypes of the centrifuges it needed to enrich uranium.

In the early years of this nuclear black market, buyers and sellers could often make simple, point-to-point transactions. A buyer would contact the seller directly, and the seller would ship items directly to the buyer. However, as the United States and Europe started trying to shut down trade in sensitive materials, countries such as Pakistan and North Korea had to come up with complicated schemes to fool the authorities. According to journalist Mark Hibbs, who helped expose Khan's network, a nuclear transaction nowadays often involves "trade brokers, shipping companies, phony bank accounts, [and] addresses for firms that don't really exist where equipment is being billed to or shipped through."[3]

For example, in a 2003 case, North Korea needed a certain type of strong aluminum pipe for building centrifuges. However, selling such materials to North Korea violates international law. So North Korea disguised the transaction. A North Korean import/export business convinced a small German company that it had been hired to supply the pipes to an aircraft plant in China. The North

MORE TO THE
STORY

THE KHAN NETWORK

A. Q. Khan became a national hero for his role in transforming Pakistan into a nuclear power. The people of his country idolized him, and the government seemed to look the other way as he went about his illegal business dealings. Khan's black market empire in nuclear technology made him immensely rich. At the height of his power, Khan owned a fleet of vintage cars, several luxury homes, and even a hotel in Timbuktu that he named after his wife. Khan was caught in 2004 when investigators found blueprints for nuclear weapons bound for Libya hidden inside bags from a dry cleaner. Khan claimed he had acted alone without the support of his government. It seems unlikely, however, that Pakistan was unaware of his activities. The government placed Khan under house arrest, but it pardoned his crimes. Khan was freed in 2009.

Korean business even supplied a document from the Chinese company that seemed official. However, customs officials caught this transaction and seized the pipes before they reached their destination, which was actually in North Korea. By the time authorities track down one of North Korea's scam companies and alert other nations not to trade with it, Hibbs says, "the North Koreans have invented a different company that's not identified because it's brand new. They set it up in some other mailbox location in some other island in the world, and they're back in business because they're operating under an identity which has not been detected."[4]

Similar to the aluminum pipes, most materials that countries need to acquire to build nuclear weapons and missiles are dual-use, meaning that nonmilitary applications exist. Hibbs explains that another method for avoiding detection involves hiding orders for sensitive materials in the midst of a long order for more mundane objects: "If you've got 150 orders for all of this junk that's supposedly useless from the point of view of a nuclear weapons program, you're going to have one or two items that are sensitive."[5] In one case, Pakistan needed steel bearings for constructing centrifuges. The country described them as parts for ballpoint pens, and it included them in an order for paper clips, wire, glue, and other items. Though in these examples officials caught the trickery, plenty of other disguised transactions have likely evaded detection. Through clever scams like these, North Korea can obtain most of the items it needs for its nuclear program without its suppliers ever realizing they have helped the regime.

DANGEROUS CUSTOMERS

Now that North Korea is a nuclear power, it has become a seller on the black market. In 2013, authorities in Panama made a surprising discovery on board a ship that had departed Cuba. They found two fighter jets, missile systems, and air defense systems hidden beneath hundreds of thousands of sacks of brown sugar, all destined for North Korea. The weapons were quite old, and Cuba said that North Korea was going to repair the weapons and then send them back. This raises the concern that North Korea could be supplying Cuba with weapons.

North Korea has also worked with Iran on nuclear technology. Reports have claimed that Iran contributed millions of dollars to North Korea's nuclear program in return for nuclear and missile technology. As of 2011, hundreds of North Korean scientists were working in Iranian nuclear plants, and Iranian scientists may have

The equipment discovered in Panama in 2013 included engines for Russian fighter jets.

attended North Korea's 2013 nuclear test. "The very first missiles we saw in Iran were simply copies of North Korean missiles," says Jeffrey Lewis of the Middlebury Institute of International Studies.[6] North Korea has also sold missiles, weapons, or related technology to Burma, Egypt, Libya, Yemen, and Syria.

NEXT-DOOR NEIGHBORS

Ever since the collapse of the Soviet Union, China has been North Korea's only ally among the major world powers. However, China has publicly denounced North Korea's nuclear tests and has even threatened sanctions against its neighbor for its provocative military actions. The two countries share an 880-mile (1,416 km) border, meaning any war or unrest in North Korea could result in a flood of refugees crossing over, a situation China wants to avoid. In addition, North Korea acts as a buffer zone between China and the US military presence in South Korea. China has a close alliance with the Kim regime, and it prefers to maintain this rather than allow the entire Korean Peninsula to come under the control of the United States and its allies. China is also interested in maintaining peace in

North Korea due to the fact that the two countries have a long-standing trading relationship.

Despite the main goal of maintaining stability in North Korea, China seems to have helped North Korea's nuclear program indirectly. First of all, China publicly supports the Kim regime, which brings some credibility to the country. Secondly, China supports the country economically. "China is currently North Korea's only economic backer of any importance," says Nicholas Eberstadt of the American

President Trump has sought the help of Chinese president Xi Jinping in handling North Korean issues.

Enterprise Institute.[7] China purchases minerals and other goods from North Korea, and it also supplies aid in the form of food and energy assistance. Without China as a trading partner, North Korea would likely be unable to finance its military activities.

Publicly, though, China seems to be distancing itself from North Korea and cooperating with the United States and the UN. China has opposed sanctions on North Korea in the past, but agreed in 2017 to halt its purchases of coal amid concerns that the money from these transactions was paying for weapons. However, analysts soon noted that coal was still getting across the border from North Korea.

Whenever the United States has considered acts of war in response to North Korea's threats, China has argued for diplomacy. In 2017, Chinese Foreign Minister Wang Yi said, "Military force cannot resolve the issue. Amid challenge there is opportunity. Amid tensions we will also find a kind of opportunity to return to talks."[8] China is hopeful the world will find a peaceful resolution to the North Korea problem.

CHAPTER SIX

FAILED
DIPLOMACY

C ountries around the world have tried a variety of diplomatic methods to convince North Korea to end its nuclear program and enter into peaceful relationships with other world powers. On several occasions, these diplomatic efforts have reached seemingly satisfactory conclusions. But over time, relationships have soured, and the countries involved have backed out of agreements or broken their promises.

TREATIES AND AGREEMENTS

North Korea's nuclear program got its start thanks to a diplomatic effort. North Korea wanted nuclear energy, supposedly for peaceful purposes, and the

Diplomatic efforts have failed to convince Kim Jong-un that he should give up North Korea's nuclear arsenal.

Soviet Union helped it build its first reactor. In 1985, the Soviet Union convinced North Korea to sign the Nuclear Nonproliferation Treaty (NPT). This treaty is intended to help prevent the use of peaceful nuclear technology to produce weapons of war. Countries that sign agree to safeguards including regular inspections of nuclear facilities. The International Atomic Energy Agency (IAEA) is the organization tasked with performing these inspections.

However, even after signing the treaty, North Korea kept finding excuses to delay inspections. When inspections finally happened in 1992, the IAEA uncovered numerous troubling signs that indicated North Korea was making plutonium for weapons. Instead of disposing of nuclear waste from its reactors, North Korea was separating out the plutonium and hiding it. In 1993, North Korea threatened to withdraw from the NPT. By 1994, the United States and North Korea were at the brink of war. The United States knew North Korea had enough plutonium to build nuclear bombs, and it felt this was an unacceptable threat. The US military made a detailed plan for an air attack to destroy the country's nuclear facilities.

MORE TO THE
STORY

SOUTH KOREA

The people of South Korea remain culturally close to the North. The countries were once one nation, and the people share a common language and culture. In addition, some families are divided, with relatives living in both the north and south. Despite these ties, South Korea is also the country most threatened by North Korea's nuclear abilities. North Korea's main goal has long been to unify the peninsula under its rule, and the country already invaded the south once. It could do so again.

Despite this threat, South Korea has led several efforts to build a friendly relationship with North Korea. During the Sunshine Policy of the late 1990s and after two important summit meetings between the leaders of the two countries in 2000 and 2007, the nations seemed to be heading toward peace. In 2004, they established the Kaesong Industrial Complex, a factory park located in North Korea but financed mainly by South Korea. The complex was intended to help boost North Korea's economy and foster a better relationship. But tensions between the two countries have grown. In 2010, the countries exchanged artillery fire, and a village on Yeonpyeong Island in South Korea was destroyed. The Kaesong facility was shut down in 2016, ending the only cooperative venture between the two nations.

Thanks to a series of diplomatic talks, the countries managed to avoid war. The talks culminated in a deal called the Agreed Framework. Under this 1994 agreement, North Korea would remain part of the NPT and cease its nuclear program. This included halting the operation of its nuclear reactors and eventually dismantling them. In return, the United States, South Korea, and Japan would build two new nuclear plants in North Korea with modern technology. These plants would produce electricity, but it would not be physically possible to use their waste to build nuclear weapons. Then, in 1998, South Korean President Kim Dae-jung implemented the Sunshine Policy, which called for cooperation and reconciliation to improve his country's relationship with the North. The relationships between North Korea and other nations seemed to be getting better.

THE AXIS OF EVIL

Soon, though, the situation worsened, and the new nuclear plants were never built. George W. Bush became president of the United States in 2001. His administration did not believe North Korea had ever intended to give up its nuclear weapons and suspected the program had continued in secret. In Bush's 2002 State of the Union address, he called Iraq, Iran, and North Korea the "axis of evil." He said, "By seeking weapons of mass destruction, these regimes pose a grave and growing danger."[1] To North Korea, these comments were both insulting and threatening. Later that year, a US envoy visiting North Korea accused the country of pursuing uranium

One year after Bush's "axis of evil" speech, the United States was at war with one of the three nations he had listed: Iraq.

enrichment. To his surprise, the North Koreans didn't try to deny it. The Agreed Framework had fallen apart.

North Korea reopened its nuclear reactors and restarted its weapons program. In 2003, North Korea became the first and only nation to withdraw from the NPT. That summer, a new diplomatic effort began. This was known as the Six-Party Talks. The talks involved China, Japan, North Korea, Russia, South Korea, and the United States. In 2005, diplomacy seemed to have won the day. In a statement, North Korea agreed to abandon all nuclear weapons and return to the NPT and IAEA safeguards, but it held onto its right to use nuclear energy. Nuclear weapons would also be removed from South Korea, and the United States stated that it had no intention to attack North Korea.

However, the very next year, North Korea tested its first nuclear weapon and a missile that could have reached the United States if it had functioned properly. The Six-Party Talks continued, but they could no longer focus on preventing North Korea from obtaining nuclear weapons since it already had them. Still, in 2007, all parties agreed to an action plan to reach the denuclearization goals that had been set in 2005, and North Korea once again shut down its nuclear power facilities. That same year, South Korea and North Korea agreed to take steps toward improved relations between the two nations. But in 2009, North Korea detonated its second nuclear bomb. Once again, diplomatic efforts continued. In early 2012, North Korea agreed to shut down its uranium enrichment plant and stop testing nuclear bombs and missiles in return for food aid from the United States. But the United States backed out of the plan after North Korea attempted to launch a satellite into space later that same year.

Since then, the situation has deteriorated. Each time North Korea has detonated a nuclear bomb, tested a missile, or launched a satellite, most of the rest of the world has responded with outrage, anger, and sanctions. Though China especially has repeatedly requested a return to the Six-Party Talks, the United States has become less inclined to negotiate. "We already don't

"SANCTIONS MEAN A WAR AND THE WAR KNOWS NO MERCY. THE US SHOULD OPT FOR DIALOGUE WITH THE DPRK, NOT FOR WAR, CLEARLY AWARE THAT IT WILL HAVE TO PAY A VERY HIGH PRICE FOR SUCH RECKLESS ACTS."[2]

—KOREAN CENTRAL NEWS AGENCY (NORTH KOREA)

have diplomatic relations; we've already sanctioned them multiple times," says David Kang of the University of Southern California.[3]

HARSH SANCTIONS

In an attempt to punish North Korea for its continued pursuit of nuclear weapons, many countries and other entities including the UN Security Council, the United States, Japan, South Korea, and the European Union (EU) have imposed sanctions. In addition, countries in the EU are not allowed to buy gold, coal, iron, diamonds, and other resources from North Korea, and North Korean banks are not allowed to operate in the EU. After North Korea's 2016 nuclear tests, the UN Security Council revised its lengthy list of sanctions, aiming to reduce the amount of money North Korea would

SUFFERING UNDER SANCTIONS

Sanctions on North Korea are meant to cripple the government and military. But they have consequences for the general population as well. For example, international aid organizations attempting to supply food, medicine, health care, and other assistance to the poor encounter difficulty running their programs. "Our projects are affected by the blocked bank transfers," says Katja Richter, who directs the North Korean branch of the German aid organization Welthungerhilfe. "International organizations here—and only a few are based in North Korea—are struggling to run their projects, and in the end the highest price [of sanctions] is paid by ordinary citizens," she says.[4]

72

make from exports by 25 percent.[5] However, North Korea seems willing to channel resources from every other area of its economy toward weaponry at the expense of its own people. "Virtually all of the DPRK's [North Korea's] resources are channeled into its reckless and relentless pursuit of weapons of mass destruction," said Samantha Power, US ambassador to the UN, in 2016.[6]

Despite the fact that harsher and harsher sanctions have been imposed with nearly every single nuclear and missile test, North Korea has not backed down. The sanctions have succeeded in crippling North Korea's economy and cementing the country's isolation from the rest of the world, but they have not prevented the development of nuclear weapons and ballistic missiles or forced a regime change. The ruling elite has been able to shield itself from the worst of the sanctions. Meanwhile, poverty among the general population has increased. Yet the people are taught to believe that their government knows what is best for them and their suffering is necessary and noble.

CHAPTER SEVEN

TAKING
HOSTAGES

North Korea has shown it is willing to go to extreme measures to get what it wants out of any international negotiation. Threatening a nuclear strike is just one strategy. Another tactic the country has routinely employed is to arrest and detain international visitors, including Americans, South Koreans, and others. These people are kept locked up in poor conditions and allowed little or no contact with the outside world. They may be forced to work and may suffer beatings or malnutrition.

Taking foreigners hostage has several advantages for North Korea. First of all, the event attracts international media coverage. This attention may force world leaders to pay attention to North Korea.

Korean American Kenneth Bae was held prisoner by North Korea for more than a year.

Secondly, hostages become bargaining chips in any international negotiations. North Korea may threaten to harm or hold onto its detainees in order to sway negotiations. Or, the country may offer to release them in return for concessions from a hostage's home country. This strategy is called hostage diplomacy. "[The hostages] are like the human shields against the US government with the ultimate goal of attention grabbing," says Koh Yu Hwan, a professor at Dongguk University in South Korea.[1]

Finally, a hostage can be useful for crafting propaganda. In several hostage situations, Kim Jong-un has claimed that his regime captured a foreign spy, whether or not the person was a real spy. The hostage is often forced to confess publicly on North Korean television. This confession is often an outright

HOSTAGE DIPLOMACY

North Korea's ruling regime isn't the only group that regularly takes hostages. Terrorist groups such as ISIS also use this strategy to garner media attention and make demands of their enemies. Many Western countries, including the United States, have implemented policies in the past stating that they will not negotiate with terrorists, especially in a hostage crisis. The idea behind such a policy is to avoid granting any recognition to the terrorist group and to make hostages less valuable for them. Also, paying a ransom for a hostage would provide money to fund the terrorist group's dangerous activities. However, in practice, many hostage crises have been resolved through negotiation. Often, each side will release one or more prisoners in an exchange that is agreeable to both sides.

lie, involving crimes that the person did not actually commit. But to those who believe it, the public confession lends credibility to the idea that Kim is a strong leader who protects his people. In the end, North Korea's Western hostages are usually let go only after a high-ranking diplomat or official visits North Korea to negotiate the release.

WHY RISK A VISIT TO NORTH KOREA?

Given the belligerent attitude of the North Korean government toward outsiders, the harsh international sanctions, and the ruling regime's humanitarian abuses, it may seem unusual that anyone would choose to travel there. But foreigners do travel in and out of North Korea. Some arrive as journalists, scholars, on business, or to take part in humanitarian efforts. But most are tourists. In fact, North Korea's tourism industry is growing. In 2014, approximately 100,000 tourists visited the country, and the regime hopes to welcome 2 million of them per year by 2020. The vast majority of these visitors come from China. However, several thousand each year come from Western nations. Tourists come for many reasons, including to run

in an annual marathon, watch military parades, or visit local attractions such as the Masikryong ski resort.

While in North Korea, foreign visitors' activities are monitored and controlled. Tourists may stay only at certain locations and are only allowed to travel accompanied by tour guides. Any misstep, such as showing disrespect for the ruling regime, could result in detainment and a harsh prison sentence. Foreigners from South Korea, Japan, and the United States have been most at risk of ending up imprisoned. The US government enacted a travel ban in September 2017 as relations between it and North Korea became strained.

TRAVEL WARNING

Before the 2017 travel ban, the US Department of State was very clear that US citizens should not travel to North Korea. However, it offered some information for people who considered going anyway. First of all, the North Korean government will not respect a visitor's privacy. The only mobile service available in the country monitors all calls. The government is also likely to search visitors' luggage, computers, and other electronic devices for any illegal items. The possession of any religious material or material critical of the North Korean government is illegal. Other illegal activities include taking unauthorized photographs, shopping at stores not intended for foreigners, and showing disrespect to North Korea's current and former leaders.

Tourists from the United States and other Western countries pose with statues of North Korea's leaders.

PRISONERS, PAST AND PRESENT

In 2009, journalists and US citizens Laura Ling and Euna Lee traveled to North Korea's border with China. They were working on a story about North Koreans who escape to China. While taking pictures, they walked out onto a frozen river that forms the border. North Korean border guards chased after the women and abducted them. They were accused of illegally entering the country and sentenced to 12 years of hard labor. Though they never wound up at a work camp, they had to confess that their goal was to overthrow the North Korean regime. Ling says, "I was told: 'If you confess, there may be forgiveness. And if you're not frank, if you don't confess, then the worst could happen.'"[2] They remained in captivity for five months. Finally, former US president Bill Clinton traveled to North Korea to secure their release.

In 2012, US citizen Kenneth Bae traveled to North Korea as a tourist. But his real goal was missionary work, which is illegal. When the authorities discovered this, he was arrested. He spent two years in captivity, the longest period of time North Korea has held an American. He was forced to work on a soybean farm. "I worked from 8 am to 6 pm at night, working on the field, carrying rock, shoveling coal," Bae says.[3] His health suffered and he lost more than 60 pounds (27 kg). However, he was allowed to communicate with his family. Bae was released in 2014 along with another American prisoner, supposedly as a gesture of good will from Kim Jong-un.

But that good will apparently didn't last. By 2017, several more Americans had been detained. One, Otto Warmbier, spent over a year as a hostage in North Korea. He died a few days after being returned home in a coma. Many believe that his death resulted from mistreatment during his imprisonment. Lee Jung Hoon, South Korea's ambassador for North Korean human rights, says that taking hostages is "immoral" and "shameless," but also very useful.[4] It helps the North Korean regime get what it wants. As tensions escalate, Lee expects that more Americans will be taken hostage.

"KIM JONG UN IS USING HOSTAGE DIPLOMACY AS A PART OF HIS MILITARY AND DEFENSE STRATEGY WITH FOCUS ON PREVENTING THE U. S. FROM REMOVING HIM FROM POWER AS WELL AS TO PREVENT THE U. S. FROM TAKING MILITARY OPTIONS AGAINST NORTH KOREA."[5]

— AN CHAN IL, PRESIDENT OF THE WORLD INSTITUTE FOR NORTH KOREA STUDIES

FROM THE
HEADLINES

A TOURIST TRIP
ENDS IN TRAGEDY

Otto Warmbier was a healthy, smart, and likable college student who planned to become an investment banker. In January 2016, he joined a tour group for a visit to North Korea. During the trip, he supposedly tried to steal a propaganda poster from a hotel. Warmbier was arrested at the airport as his group was preparing to leave the country. Danny Gratton, a citizen of the United Kingdom who participated in the same tour, believes that Warmbier did not commit any crime and was just "in the wrong place at the wrong time."[6]

Warmbier was sentenced to 15 years of hard labor and forced to confess publicly for his alleged crimes. In February 2016, he appeared on North Korean television and said that he tried to steal the sign in order to "harm the work ethic and motivation of the Korean people."[7] It's unclear what happened to Warmbier over the following year. In June 2017, the North Korean government sent him home—in a coma. He was unable to see, speak, or respond to verbal commands. He died a few days after arriving in the United States. His family is convinced that his death resulted from mistreatment during his long imprisonment.

Warmbier was marched before a microphone and forced to confess for his supposed crimes.

82

CHAPTER EIGHT

AN UNCERTAIN FUTURE

T he government of North Korea continues to survive against all odds. Experts have predicted the regime's demise many times in the past, especially during periods of crisis. But it has survived the collapse of the Soviet Union, famine, and two transfers of power within the Kim family. It has also survived increasingly harsh sanctions that have crippled the economy.

Eventually, though, something could happen to trigger a change. But no one knows whether the change would be gradual or quick, peaceful or violent. The best-case scenario might be a peaceful transfer of power or a transformation of the current regime to a more open, flexible government willing to give

In 2017, the eyes of the world were trained on Pyongyang, the capital of secretive North Korea, watching for signs of a worsening crisis.

up nuclear weapons and properly care for its people. This seems unlikely given the current situation. More likely scenarios include a forced regime change due to revolution, a foreign invasion, or armed conflict. Each of these scenarios could potentially lead to nuclear war, the worst-case scenario. For this reason, policy experts are treading carefully as they consider methods of responding to the threat posed by North Korea's nuclear program. The choices made now will determine which potential future becomes reality.

REGIME CHANGE

Many experts in the United States argue that diplomacy with the current North Korean government has run its course, and that the regime must change before the nuclear threat will go away. Nicholas Eberstadt of the American Enterprise Institute says: "For over 20 years, I've been arguing that the North Korean nuclear problem is the North Korean regime, and we won't have denuclearization until we have a better class of dictator there."[1] Sue Mi Terry, who formerly worked for the Central Intelligence Agency as a senior analyst on North Korea, agrees. "I really don't think that the regime could be persuaded to give up its nuclear program," she says.[2]

Even though many countries would love to see new leadership in North Korea, many believe that regime change can't happen without a period of instability and violence, which could lead to a situation in which the country's nuclear weapons are up for grabs for anyone to commandeer. In April 2017, US secretary of state Rex Tillerson said, "Our goal is not regime change, nor do we desire to threaten the North Korean people or destabilize the Asia Pacific region."[3] In the past, the main strategy for the United States has been to sit back and wait. Eventually, the regime might change on its own or at least decide to end the nuclear program. Former President Barack Obama called this "strategic patience."[4] By 2017, the new

Tillerson, *center*, was accompanied by US troops to the village that serves as a meeting point for North and South Korean negotiators.

presidential administration took a new approach, as North Korea continued its weapons and missile tests. "The era of strategic patience is over," Vice President Mike Pence said.[5] There are several ways the United States and its allies could attempt to steer North Korea toward a friendlier form of government.

UPHEAVAL FROM WITHIN

One of the strategies experts suggest is to continue to tighten sanctions to exert pressure on North Korea until it collapses on its own. There are several ways such a collapse could occur, and each is problematic. One would be a military takeover, in which the already powerful North Korean military deposes Kim Jong-un and takes control. However, there's no guarantee that a military government in North Korea would be any friendlier than the current leadership. It might simply continue to threaten the rest of the world with nuclear strikes. Some have suggested a covert operation by outside governments to engineer a coup. They could do this by convincing a group of North Korean generals to overthrow the Kim family and install a friendly government. China would be the country most likely to be able to accomplish this feat due to its historically close relationship with North Korea. But China's ties to North Korea aren't as strong as they once were. Plus, North Korea seems willing to assassinate anyone who seems like a potential threat to the current leadership—even family members. Kim Jong-un's half-brother Kim Jong-nam was killed in a poison attack in Malaysia in February 2017.

Another possible avenue of collapse is a popular uprising. These sorts of regime changes swept through several countries in the Middle East and North Africa in the early 2010s, in what became known as the Arab Spring. However, it seems unlikely that the people of North Korea will rebel against their leaders. In more than 70 years of

DEFECTORS

Refugees, who become known as defectors, have been escaping from North Korea since the end of the Korean War. Almost all of them flee by crossing the border into China. The number of escapees rose steadily from the late 1990s through the 2000s. In 2007, a record high of 2,914 people left.[6] But the number dropped again after Kim Jong-un took power. He toughened border controls and imposed harsher punishments for people trying to flee. Defectors who get caught may be thrown into jail, sent to a work camp, or even executed. China also has a policy of trying to keep refugees out and sending those who cross back to North Korea. Despite the risks, the number of defectors started rising once again in 2016. Among defectors fleeing due to hunger and poverty are a growing number of people leaving for political or social reasons.

FROM THE
HEADLINES

PUBLIC POISONING

It sounds like the plot of a spy novel: two women walk up to a man standing by a check-in kiosk at the airport. They grab him and press their poison-coated hands against his face. He soon begins feeling dizzy, then dies 20 minutes later. But this is no fictional story. This public assassination actually happened at Kuala Lumpur International Airport in Malaysia on February 13, 2017. The man, Kim Jong-nam, was the eldest son of the former dictator of North Korea, Kim Jong-il, and half-brother of the current leader, Kim Jong-un. The assassins used VX nerve agent, an extremely deadly substance that is considered a chemical weapon and whose use has been banned under several international agreements.

Many suspect that North Korea ordered the killing, though this connection has not been proven. "The fact that so many North Korean agents were involved shows that the operation was planned well in advance and was done with Kim Jong-un's blessing," said Sue Mi Terry, a former CIA analyst.[7] It's possible that Kim Jong-un thought his sibling might try to take power in a coup or regime change. Terry went on to say that Kim Jong-un may have been worried that China or the United States would try

Crews in protective suits cleaned the airport in Kuala Lumpur following the assassination of Kim Jong-nam.

to install Kim Jong-nam as the leader in North Korea. The Kim family has a long history of killing people to eliminate potential opposition. If North Korea is indeed responsible, the use of VX demonstrates how little the country cares about global laws and norms.

dictatorship, the country has never had an internal revolt. The personality cult is deeply entrenched. People may genuinely believe that their leaders are doing a good job. After all, they have almost no access to news of the outside world. Or, they may be too fearful of the repercussions should they rebel. The Kim regime quells any opposition with public executions or prison sentences in grueling work camps. In addition, many people in North Korea are poor and starving. They may be too busy trying to survive to organize any sort of opposition.

Rather than taking action to overthrow the government, the people may become desperate enough to attempt to flee in large numbers. One group that promotes this approach to solving the problem is the North Korea Freedom Coalition. Organizer Michael Horowitz says his group "seeks the implosion of the regime without a shot being fired."[8] The group believes making it easier for North Korean refugees to immigrate to the United States will prompt many more people to leave. The US government, though, worries that the regime might use such a program to send away criminals or sick people, or even to install spies in the United States.

A MILITARY STRIKE

The most direct approach to installing a new regime in

North Korea would be military action. The United States

is the country most likely to lead a military strike against

North Korea, and it has already taken steps to prepare

should such action be necessary. The THAAD missile

US forces in South Korea frequently hold drills to demonstrate their strength and readiness.

defense system is in place in South Korea, and US warships are stationed nearby. The United States has used military action to solve problems in the past. The 2003 US invasion of Iraq toppled dictator Saddam Hussein. A special-forces raid killed terrorist leader Osama Bin Laden in 2011. A South Korean newspaper even claimed in March 2017 that this same special-forces team was in South Korea for military drills to practice removing Kim Jong-un. However, the United States denied this was true.

A more likely military approach would be targeted US strikes on key parts of the North Korean nuclear and missile infrastructure, such as its ballistic missile production facilities or ballistic missile command centers. However, many of these facilities are well hidden, so there's no guarantee that such a preemptive strike would disable North Korea completely. The attack would almost certainly prompt Kim Jong-un to strike back against Seoul, the capital of South Korea, potentially killing millions of people. Seoul lies just across the border from North Korea, within easy reach of short-range missiles and artillery. As a result, South Koreans generally oppose any military action. Thae Yong-ho, who served as the North Korean ambassador to the United Kingdom before he defected in 2016, says a military strike while Kim Jong-un is still in power is a bad idea. He says, "North Korea's leader won't back off. A preemptive strike against North Korea will bring about a huge catastrophe."[9]

War could also break out if North Korea decides to launch a preemptive nuclear strike against the United States or South Korea. This seems unlikely, though. Many experts feel that North Korea developed its nuclear weapons mainly as a deterrent, meaning it built them to discourage the United States or other nations from attacking. Still, it's hard to predict the actions of a dictator. Thae has also said, "I think that Kim Jong-un will press the button [to fire a nuclear weapon] if his rule and his dynasty are threatened."[10] In addition, if war seems

WAR GAMES

Military officials and public policy experts occasionally participate in war games to act out scenarios that might occur in a real conflict. In 2005, Sam Gardiner, a retired US Air Force colonel, ran a war game about the situation in North Korea. To take out all of the missile sites and nuclear sites before North Korea would have a chance to use them, he said, the United States would need to run 4,000 air missions per day. This seemed impossible to Jessica Matthews, who formerly worked for the State Department. She said, "My understanding is that we cannot protect Seoul, at least for the first twenty-four hours of a war. . . . There are a hundred thousand Americans in Seoul, not to mention ten million South Koreans."[11]

likely to break out, North Korea may place some of its missiles on alert, meaning that they are ready to launch within minutes. These weapons could potentially fire off accidentally or without official approval.

The best chance for a peaceful resolution to the situation in North Korea would likely be diplomatic engagement. That means talking to Kim Jong-un and

When President Obama left office, he advised incoming President Trump that North Korea would be one of his most challenging foreign policy concerns.

coming to some sort of mutual understanding in which the current regime stops threatening the rest of the world. Siegfried Hecker, a nuclear scientist who has visited North Korea multiple times, explains that waiting patiently is no longer an option. In addition, he says, "A military attack is out of the question. Tightening sanctions further is likewise a dead end, particularly given the advances made in their nuclear program. . . . The only hope appears to be engagement."[12]

Engagement isn't an attractive option, though, given North Korea's past record of coming to agreements, then continuing on with its nuclear program in secret. There is also a moral dilemma in trying to establish a friendly relationship with a dictator who has terrorized his people. Wendy Sherman, who served as the US Undersecretary of State for Political Affairs, says that Kim "is a leader who has left his people with no freedom, no choices, no food, no future. People are executed. There are labor camps. But the decision we have to make is whether to try to deal with him to open the country so that the people of North Korea do have freedom, do have choices, do have food."[13]

Humanitarian aid is one bargaining chip the United States and other countries have used in the past and may use again. In a way, this is the opposite of sanctions. Rather than taking something away to punish the regime, aid is like reaching out a hand to offer assistance, but assistance that comes at a price. North Korea would probably have to take action to dismantle its nuclear program in order to receive the aid. In 2016, John Kerry, US secretary of state at the time, said, "We have made overture after overture to the dictator of North Korea. . . . We have made it very clear to him that we're prepared to talk about peace, about peace on the peninsula, about food assistance, about normal relationship with the world, about a nonaggression pact . . . if he will simply acknowledge he is prepared to come to the table and talk about denuclearization and his responsibilities to the world."[14]

Most likely, the only way that engagement will make any progress is if the negotiators manage to convince North Korea that its existence is no longer at stake. In order to give up nuclear weapons, North Korea's leadership may need to no longer feel as though it needs them for protection or as a key piece of its national identity. In the past, countries have only given up their nuclear weapons when political disputes have been completely resolved. Yet the history of US government attitudes toward North Korea make it unlikely that the regime would believe it is completely safe. Ridding the world of the threat posed by a nuclear North Korea would probably require resolving the conflict between North and South Korea while taking into account the interests of the United States, China, and Japan. This will not be easy to accomplish. Every potential solution to the problem with North Korea has drawbacks. By 2017, no good answer was apparent. The world could only hope that the issue would be resolved in a manner that does not result in a catastrophe.

ESSENTIAL
FACTS

MAJOR EVENTS

- In 2003, North Korea withdrew from a treaty intended to stop the spread of nuclear weapons. It was the first and only country ever to do so.

- In 2006, North Korea successfully tested its first nuclear weapon.

- In 2011, North Korean dictator Kim Jong-il died. His son, Kim Jong-un, took power.

- In 2016, North Korea tested two nuclear weapons. It claimed the first one was a hydrogen bomb. However, experts disputed this claim.

- In 2017, in response to recent North Korean missile tests, the United States and South Korea established an advanced missile defense system in South Korea.

- In 2017, North Korea successfully launched its first intercontinental ballistic missile.

KEY PLAYERS

- Kim Jong-un is the third member of the Kim family to lead North Korea. The Kim regime has absolute power over the country and has established a personality cult.

- US President Donald Trump faced increasing tensions with North Korea upon taking office in 2017.

IMPACT ON SOCIETY

North Korea's weapons pose a threat to the safety and security of the world. The country has tested nuclear bombs and missiles in violation of international law, claiming it needs nuclear weapons to defend itself from its enemies. By 2017 North Korea had the capability to strike South Korea and Japan. It was developing intercontinental ballistic missiles that would allow it to strike the mainland of the United States. To respond to this threat, world leaders are trying different tactics, including attempting to open diplomatic negotiations, imposing sanctions, and preparing for the possibility of war.

QUOTE

"Far from achieving its stated national security and economic development goals, North Korea's provocative and destabilizing actions have instead served to isolate and impoverish its people through its relentless pursuit of nuclear weapons and ballistic missile capabilities."

—President Barack Obama, September 2016

GLOSSARY

CENTRIFUGE

A machine that rapidly rotates in order to separate materials of different densities. A special kind of centrifuge is used to enrich uranium for nuclear energy or nuclear weapons.

DICTATOR

A leader who has complete control over a country.

INTERCONTINENTAL BALLISTIC MISSILE

A weapon that flies under its own power and uses a guidance system to strike a specific target at long range.

ISOTOPE

A form of an element with a differing number of neutrons in its nucleus.

PERSONALITY CULT

The treatment of a leader as an idealized figure to be worshiped.

PLUTONIUM

A metal that is produced as waste in certain nuclear reactors and can also be used as fuel for nuclear weapons.

PROLIFERATION

A rapid spreading or increase; often referring to the spread of nuclear weapons.

PROPAGANDA

Information that carries facts or details slanted to favor a single point of view or political bias.

REGIME

The government in control of a country.

SANCTION

An action taken to punish a country or force it to follow international laws.

ADDITIONAL
RESOURCES

SELECTED BIBLIOGRAPHY

Cha, Victor. *The Impossible State: North Korea, Past and Future*. New York: Ecco, 2012. Print.

Chang, Gordon G. *Nuclear Showdown: North Korea Takes on the World*. New York: Random, 2006. Print.

French, Paul. *North Korea: State of Paranoia*. New York: Zed, 2014. Print.

FURTHER READINGS

Foran, Racquel. *North Korea*. Minneapolis, MN: Abdo, 2013. Print.

Foran, Racquel. *South Korea*. Minneapolis, MN: Abdo, 2013. Print.

Freese, Susan M. *Nuclear Weapons*. Minneapolis, MN: Abdo, 2012. Print.

ONLINE RESOURCES

Booklinks
NONFICTION NETWORK
FREE! ONLINE NONFICTION RESOURCES

To learn more about North Korea today, visit
abdobooklinks.com. These links are routinely monitored and
updated to provide the most current information available.

MORE INFORMATION

For more information on this subject, contact or visit the
following organizations:

International Atomic Energy Agency (IAEA)
Vienna International Centre, PO Box 100
A-1400 Vienna, Austria
+431 2600-0
iaea.org
The IAEA is responsible for promoting peaceful and safe uses for nuclear
technology, such as in power plants.

The Nuclear Threat Initiative (NTI)
1747 Pennsylvania Avenue NW
Seventh Floor
Washington, DC 20006
202-296-4810
nti.org
The NTI works to prevent catastrophic attacks with weapons of mass
destruction and disruption, including nuclear weapons, chemical weapons,
cyberattacks, and more.

SOURCE
NOTES

CHAPTER 1. BOMB THREAT

1. Choe Sang-Hun. "North Korean Propaganda Video Depicts Nuclear Strike on Washington." *New York Times*. New York Times, 26 Mar. 2016. Web. 13 Apr. 2017.

2. Anna Fifield. "North Korea Claims It Could Wipe Out Manhattan." *Washington Post*. Washington Post, 13 Mar. 2016. Web. 13 Apr. 2017.

3. Jack Kim. "N. Korea Leader Tells Military to Be Ready to Use Nuclear Weapons." *Reuters*. Reuters, 7 Mar. 2016. Web. 13 Apr. 2017.

4. "How Potent Are NK's Threats?" *BBC*. BBC, 15 Sept. 2015. Web. 13 Apr. 2017.

5. "NK Admits to Having Nukes." *Seattle Times*. Seattle Times, 10 Feb. 2005. Web. 13 Apr. 2017.

6. "Types of Nuclear Weapons." *CTBTO*. CTBTO, n.d. Web. 13 Apr. 2017.

7. David E. Sanger. "As North Korea Speeds Its Nuclear Program, US Fears Time Will Run Out." *New York Times*. New York Times, 24 Apr. 2017. Web. 4 May 2017.

8. Michelle Nichols and Lesley Wroughton. "US Says Time to Act on North Korea." *Reuters*. Reuters, 28 Apr. 2017. Web. 4 May 2017.

9. Barack Obama. "Statement by the President on North Korea's Nuclear Test." *White House*. White House, 9 Sept. 2016. Web. 18 Aug. 2017.

10. "US Warship Starts Drill with South Korea amid Tensions with North." *Press TV*. Press TV, 2017. Web. 18 Aug. 2017.

11. Tim Schwarz. "North Korea Issues Warning as US Strike Group Heads to Korean Peninsula." *CNN*. CNN, 13 Apr. 2017. Web. 18 Aug. 2017.

CHAPTER 2. A NUCLEAR WORLD

1. Carl Sagan. "'The Day After' Nuclear War/Deterrence Discussion Panel." *ABC News Viewpoint*. YouTube, 20 Nov. 1983. Web. 18 Aug. 2017.

CHAPTER 3. THE ROGUE STATE

1. Mina Yoon. "Who Do North Koreans Think Started the Korean War?" NKNews.org. NKNews.org, 8 Jan. 2014. Web. 4 May 2017.

2. Zack Beauchamp. "A Brief History of North Korea's Nuclear Program and the Failed US Campaign to Stop It." *Vox*. Vox, 7 Jan. 2016. Web. 11 May 2017.

3. Mina Yoon. "Who Do North Koreans Think Started the Korean War?" NKNews.org. NKNews.org, 8 Jan. 2014. Web. 4 May 2017.

4. Gordon G. Chang. *Nuclear Showdown*. New York: Random, 2006. Print. 10.

5. Christopher Richardson. "Hagiography of the Kims & the Childhood of Saints: Kim Il-Sung." *Sino NK*. Sino NK, 31 Jan. 2015. Web. 4 May 2017.

6. Victor Cha. *The Impossible State*. New York: Ecco, 2012. Print. 90.

7. "How North Korea Children Are Taught to Hate the 'American B*******' at Kindergarten." *Daily Mail*. Daily Mail, 23 June 2012. Web. 4 May 2017.

8. Gordon C. Chang. *Nuclear Showdown*. New York: Random, 2006. Print. 4.

9. Tom Phillips. "Escape from North Korea: 'How I Escaped Horrors of Life under Kim Jong-Il." *Telegraph*. Telegraph, 11 Nov. 2014. Web. 4 May 2017.

10. Sara Malm. "Kim Jong-un Warns North Koreans." *Daily Mail*. Daily Mail. 30 Mar. 2016. Web. 11 May 2017.

11. "North Korea." *Global Hunger Index*. GHI, 2016. Web. 4 May 2017.

12. Robertson. "NK's Caste System." *HRW*. HRW, 5 July 2016. Web. 18 Aug. 2017.

13. Victor Cha. *The Impossible State*. New York: Ecco, 2012. Print. 173.

14. Robertson. "NK's Caste System." *HRW*. HRW, 5 July 2016. Web. 18 Aug. 2017.

CHAPTER 4. MILITARY MIGHT

1. David E. Sanger. "As North Korea's Nuclear Program Advances, US Strategy Is Tested." *New York Times*. New York Times, 6 May 2016. Web. 8 May 2017.

2. Scott Stossel. "The War Game." *Atlantic*. Atlantic, 2005. Web. 13 May 2017.

3. David E. Sanger. "As North Korea Speeds Its Nuclear Program, US Fears Time Will Run Out." *New York Times*. New York Times, 24 Apr. 2017. Web. 4 May 2017.

4. Richard Harris. "Did North Korea Test a 'Miniature' Nuclear Bomb?" *NPR*. NPR, 12 Feb. 2013. Web. 8 May 2017.

5. Ralph Savelsberg and James Kiessling. "North Korea's Musudan Missile: A Performance Assessment." *38 North*. 38 North, 20 Dec. 2016. Web. 8 May 2017.

6. Kyle Mizokami. "How Far Can North Korea's Missiles Really Go?" *Popular Mechanics*. Popular Mechanics, 20 Sept. 2016. Web. 18 Aug. 2017.

7. David Sanger. "The US Has an 'Active Cyber War Underway' to Thwart the North Korean Nuclear Threat." *Fresh Air*. NPR, 29 Mar. 2017. Web. 8 May 2017.

8. Anna Fifield. "North Korea Launches 'Satellite.'" *Washington Post*. Washington Post, 6 Feb. 2016. Web. 8 May 2017.

9. "UN Chief Calls on DPR Korea to Halt 'Provocative Actions' Following Missile Launch." *UN News Centre*. UN, 7 Feb. 2016. Web. 8 May 2017.

10. Richard Harris. "Did North Korea Test a 'Miniature' Nuclear Bomb?" *NPR*. NPR, 12 Feb. 2013. Web. 8 May 2017.

11. Jonathan Kaiman. "Here's What's Driving North Korea's Nuclear Program." *Los Angeles Times*. Los Angeles Times, 1 May 2017. Web. 8 May 2017.

SOURCE NOTES
CONTINUED

12. "Kim Jong-un Oversees Display of N Korea Military Force." *Al Jazeera*. Al Jazeera, 15 Apr. 2017. Web. 8 May 2017.

13. Choe Sang-Hun. "US Confirms North Korea Fired Intercontinental Ballistic Missile." *New York Times*. New York Times, 4 July 2017. Web. 18 Aug. 2017.

14. "Statement by Secretary Tillerson." *US Department of State*. US Department of State, 4 July 2017. Web. 18 Aug. 2017.

CHAPTER 5. A SECRET MARKET

1. "Syria: The Story of the Conflict." *BBC*. BBC, 11 Mar. 2016. Web. 11 May 2017.

2. William J. Broad, et al. "A Tale of Nuclear Proliferation: How Pakistani Built His Network." *New York Times*. New York Times, 12 Feb. 2004. Web. 9 May 2017.

3. Armin Rosen. "How NK Built Its Nuclear Program." *Atlantic*. Atlantic, 10 Apr. 2013. Web. 13 Apr. 2017.

4. Ibid.

5. Ibid.

6. Harry Walker. "Iran and North Korea 'Sharing Expertise on Ballistic Missiles' Amid Tensions with the US." *Express*. Express, 6 May 2017. Web. 11 May 2017.

7. Eleanor Albert. "The China–North Korea Relationship." *Council on Foreign Relations*. CFR, 26 Apr. 2017. Web. 11 May 2017.

8. Greg Price. "Why China Remains North Korea's Biggest Ally." *Newsweek*. Newsweek, 13 Apr. 2017. Web. 11 May 2017.

CHAPTER 6. FAILED DIPLOMACY

1. Jamie Fuller. "Axis of Evil." *Washington Post*. WP, 25 Jan. 2014. 13 May 2017.

2. "NK's 'Sanctions' Attack." *BBC News*. BBC, 7 Jan. 2003. Web. 18 Aug. 2017.

3. Zack Beauchamp. "A Brief History of North Korea's Nuclear Program and the Failed US Campaign to Stop It." *Vox*. Vox, 7 Jan. 2016. Web. 11 May 2017.

4. Fragkiska Megaloudi. "North Korea: Sanctions, Luxury, and Aid." *Al Jazeera*. Al Jazeera, 13 May 2014. Web. 11 May 2017.

5. Yeganeh Torbati. "US Readying New North Korea Sanctions if Needed: Tillerson." *Reuters.* Reuters, 3 May 2017. Web. 11 May 2017.

6. Serina Sandhu. "China Announces Sanctions against North Korea." *Independent.* Independent, 5 Apr. 2016. Web. 11 May 2017.

CHAPTER 7. TAKING HOSTAGES

1. Kim. "NK's Hostage Diplomacy." *NBC.* NBC, 8 May 2017. Web. 18 Aug. 2017.

2. "Surviving North Korea." *Oprah.* Oprah, 18 May 2010. Web. 12 July 2017.

3. Rachel Clarke. "What Happens to Americans Detained in North Korea?" *CNN.* CNN, 8 May 2017. Web. 12 July 2017.

4. Stella Kim and Saphora Smith. "North Korea's 'Hostage Diplomacy': Kim Uses Detained Americans as Leverage." *NBC News.* NBC, 8 May 2017. Web. 18 Aug. 2017.

5. Ibid.

6. Kevin Ponniah and Tom Spender. "Otto Warmbier: How Did North Korea Holiday End in Jail, and a Coma?" *BBC News.* BBC, 20 June 2017. Web. 12 July 2017.

7. Ibid.

CHAPTER 8. AN UNCERTAIN FUTURE

1. Lee. "Trump Reviews Policy on NK." *VOA.* VOA, 3 Feb. 2017. Web. 13 May 2017.

2. Ibid.

3. Max Greenwood. "Tillerson on North Korea: 'Our Goal Is Not Regime Change.'" *Hill.* Hill, 28 Apr. 2017. Web. 13 May 2017.

4. Scott A. Snyder. "US Policy Toward North Korea." *Council on Foreign Relations.* CFR, Jan. 2013. Web. 13 May 2017.

5. "North Korea on 'Maximum Alert' after US Threats." *Al Jazeera.* Al Jazeera, 17 Apr. 2017. Web. 13 May 2017.

6. Tae-woo Kim. "Number of Elite North Korean Defectors on the Rise." *Diplomat.* Diplomat, 19 Aug. 2016. Web. 13 May 2017.

7. Anna Fifield. "For Kim Jong Nam, a Sad Ending to a Lonely Life." *Washington Post.* Washington Post, 24 Feb. 2017. Web. 13 May 2017.

8. Paul French. *North Korea: State of Paranoia.* New York: Zed, 2014. Print. 394.

9. Ross Logan. "Defector Says Pre-Emptive Strikes Would Create 'Huge Catastrophe.'" *Sunday Express.* Sunday Express, 10 Feb. 2017. Web. 13 May 2017.

10. Ryan Pickrell. "Why Would North Korea Launch a Nuclear Missile?" *National Interest.* National Interest, 24 Apr. 2017. Web. 13 May 2017.

11. Scott Stossel. "The War Game." *Atlantic.* Atlantic, 2005. Web. 13 May 2017.

12. Siegfried S. Hecker. "A Return Trip to North Korea's Yongbyon Nuclear Complex." *NAPSNet Special Reports.* Nautilus, 22 Nov. 2010. Web. 4 May 2017.

13. Paul French. *North Korea: State of Paranoia.* New York: Zed, 2014. Print. 421.

14. Eli Lake. "Preparing for North Korea's Inevitable Collapse." *Bloomberg.* Bloomberg, 20 Sept. 2016. Web. 13 May 2017.

15. Lee. "Trump Reviews Policy on NK." *VOA.* VOA, 3 Feb. 2017. Web. 13 May 2017.

INDEX

ABOUT THE
AUTHOR

Kathryn Hulick is a freelance writer and former Peace Corps volunteer. After returning from two years teaching English in Kyrgyzstan, she started writing for children. Her recent published books include a Special Reports title, *Fracking*. She also contributes regularly to *Muse* magazine and the *Science News for Students* website. She enjoys hiking, painting, reading, and working in her garden. She lives in Massachusetts with her husband, son, and dog.